The Mysterious Star

Storyline **Shirley Ann Freed**
Illustrations **Steven Butler**

One night, some wise men saw a bright star.

It was a new star. They had never seen it before!

They found other wise men. "Look at the new star!"

"Where did it come from? What does it mean?"

No one knew. It was a mystery.

The wise men read their ancient scrolls.

Every night they looked at the mysterious star.

What did it mean? No one knew. It was a mystery.

The wise men read more. They finally understood.

The star was a sign that a great king was born!

One night while they looked, the star began to move!

The wise men decided to follow the star.

Night after night they followed the mysterious star.

Day after day they read their ancient scrolls.

The star led to Jerusalem, but no one there
had seen the star.

The priests were working as usual.
They had not seen the sign.

King Herod was not happy to hear about the star.

He was not happy to hear about another king.

"Where is the child?" King Herod demanded.

"He will be born in Bethlehem," said the priests.

The wise men followed the star to find Jesus.

It stopped over the house where Jesus was.

The wise men were happy. They'd followed the mysterious star and found the son of God.